IN WESTON SKIES

Dreoilín

IN WESTON SKIES

A personal memoir of flying at Weston in the 1950's

Bob Montgomery

BY THE SAME AUTHOR

The 1903 Irish Gordon Bennett - The Race that Saved Motor Sport
An Irish Roadside Camera 1896-1906
Down Many a Road: The Story of Shell in Ireland 1921-2002
An Irish Roadside Camera 1907-1918
Racing in the Park: 100 Years of Motor Racing in the Phoenix Park
An Irish Roadside Camera 1919-1939
A Lifetimes Collecting: The Legendary Car Collection of Jim Boland
Great Drives: 22 Great Irish Roads
An Eclectic Eye: the photographs of TW Murphy
Drive Ireland

Dreoilin Transport Albums
Early Motoring in Ireland
Leslie Porter - Ireland's Pioneer Racing Driver
The Irish Grand Prix 1929-1931
The Phoenix Park Speed Trials 1903
The Irish Gordon Bennett Race 1903
Ford Manufacture and Assembly at Cork 1919-1984
RJ Mecredy: The Father of Irish Motoring
The Royal Irish Automobile Club
Early Aviation in Ireland
Irish Motor Racing Circuits - Volume 1
Motor Assembly in Ireland

Front cover: Vincent Killowry's fine painting of my father's Tiger Moth (EI-AHJ) over Weston Aerodrome in the mid 1950s.

Club members in front of the Weston Limited DH Rapide photographed in 1955.
1 2 3 Unknown 4 George Donohoe 5 David Montgomery 6 Stephen Donohoe 7 Cormac Murray 8 Unknown 9 Richard Kennedy 10 Unknown 11 Frank Murray 12 Son of Ernie Verso 13 Barbara Kennedy 14 Son of Ernie Verso 15 Unknown 16 Roger Kennedy 17 Paul Martin 18 19 Unknown 20 Thomas Keogh 21 John Neill 22 Kevin Murray 23 Tom Mulock 24 Ken Brown 25 Jack Louth 26 Bob Stewart 27 Unknown 28 Ciaran Quinn 29 Judy Lyons 30 31 Unknown 32 Tom Dean 33 Ernie Verso 34 Bob Levis 35 Cyril Murray 36 Unknown 37 Bob Montgomery 38 Pearse Cahill 39 Nat Preston 40 Wilford Fitzsimmons 41 42 Unknown 43 Ken Smith 44 John O'Dea 45 Rosemary Kennedy 46 Darby Kennedy 47 Pat O'Hara

FOREWORD

I am delighted and honoured to have been asked by Bob Montgomery to write the foreword for this book.My introduction to Weston Aerodrome came about as a result of an article published in the *Sunday Press* in 1955 entitled 'The little boy who watches aeroplanes go by'. The article highlighted my frequent weekend visits to Dublin Airport at the age of eleven. David Montgomery, Bob's father, who was secretary of the Aero Club of Ireland took an interest in this article and contacted the *Sunday Press* offering to bring me to Weston for a flight in his aeroplane and use the opportunity for a follow-up article in their newspaper. I recall being escorted by my mother to David's hardware premises in Parnell Street and from there to Weston for my first flight. I clearly remember David as being a very tall and pleasant man who put me at ease from the very beginning.

Getting airborne for the first time was an amazing experience and something I will never forget. We flew around the Maynooth area in a BA Swallow aircraft registration EI-AGA and we were joined afterwards by an Auster EI-AGJ flown by the legendary 'Monkey' Morgan flying in tight formation with us for air-to-air photographs. I already had a significant interest in aeroplanes prior to this, however my flight with David left me in no doubt as to what would be my career of choice and for this I will be forever grateful to David.

In the weeks that followed I met David on the odd visit to Weston and my memory is that of a man deeply committed to imparting knowledge about the theory of flight to groups of interested people who would gather around his aircraft. He was clearly passionate about the wonders of flight and was keen to engage with others to share this passion. Unfortunately, my friendship with David was all too short. The news of his tragic death at Lucan was devastating and is still much in my memory.

Some years later in 1964 I began taking flying lessons at Weston with the Leinster Aero Club, formerly the Aero Club of Ireland, with dedicated instructors like Denis Leonard, Paddy Robinson and Bill Howarth. Thanks to Weston, and, in particular, David Montgomery, for playing such a significant role in the promotion of Irish aviation and for being an important element in my aviation career.

Michael O'Brien,
August 2018.

INTRODUCTION

Memories of a golden childhood and of the events that shaped so much of my life and the lives of others prompted me at last to write this book. It's a book I always intended to write, but like so many of us and our intentions, until now, life simply got in the way. Perhaps, that was no bad thing, for now I can bring a greater perspective to my parent's story and the significance of all those days spent flying at Weston.

Despite the tragedy that befell my father and his pupil, William Kenny, my memories of Weston are good and I'm extremely grateful for them. What young boy would not have relished the opportunity to have Weston as a playground and to fly every week in such aircraft as the Tiger Moth or the graceful Swallow? A shy child, I came into my own at Weston and apart from the flying memories, I can recall being towed around sitting on a sack behind an ex-army tender driven at speed by Darby Kennedy's sons, horse-riding and walks with my mother to the 'lake', the spot where the River Liffey broadened out and was a landmark for fliers returning to Weston Aerodrome.

In writing this account I had the help of two invaluable sources: my father's photographs and also the notes that he wrote each week about Aero Club of Ireland activities and that appeared in the *Evening Mail*, the Dublin evening newspaper. These notes are a mine of information and helped me to correct where my memory misled me.

So then, what follows is a celebration of Weston in the 1950s when it was the centre of a revival of private aviation in Ireland – something recorded in my father's own photogaphs and in his collection of photographs taken by others at the time – when the Weston Air Displays were the event that inspired many aviation careers, and that even today, are remembered vividly by those who were there as young boys and girls.

So, sit back and enjoy this flight though a long-gone period of flying in Ireland, surely a golden time when aviation was simpler and free of many of the restrictions that are necessary today. Happy landings!

Bob Montgomery
August 2018

DEDICATION

For my parents, Aviators both.

There are no skies like Irish skies
George Bernard Shaw

When once you have tasted flight, you will forever walk the earth with your eyes turned skyward,
for there you have been, and there you will always long to return.
Leonardo da Vinci

Silver wings on an Autumn day
Took you away from me.
BM

A PASSION FOR FLYING

Sunday 30th September 1956 promised to be a good day. The weather was suitable for flying and on arrival at Weston aerodrome everything looked good for the 'At Home' the Aero Club of Ireland was due to hold there that afternoon. As we - my father, mother, and sister Ruth - drove into the airfield there was a large collection of aircraft parked in various stages of preparation for the day's activities. These would include a cross-country competition for the Club's pilots and their guests, for every member was expected to bring along at least one potential new member who would hopefully enjoy the friendly atmosphere and might subsequently join the Club.

As always, I was looking forward to flying with my father, David, or 'Dave' as he was known to all in his role as the energetic and enthusiastic Honorary Secretary of the Club. But before we got to the afternoons activities, there was another task to be completed. Since before the Second World War, when 'Darby' Kennedy had established Weston Limited, and begun flying from the County Kildare aerodrome, Weston had been the centre of private flying activity in the State. It had weathered many financial storms during this time and Darby's attempts to found an airline in competition to the State airline, Aer Lingus, had been continually thwarted by Government. Now, it faced a different crisis as it looked as if it might be lost as a flying site. This was potentially very bad news for the Aero Club of Ireland that had used Weston as its base since being formed a few years previously in May 1953, and also for the Irish Parachute Club that had been formed only weeks earlier and that planned to use Weston as its base for operations. As a result, the Club began to seek alternative sites at which to develop a new flying site and where they could base themselves.

Today, it was planned that George Donohoe, a prominent member of the Club and a close friend of my father, would join us in flying to view a suggested site for a flying field. George was to fly in his BA Swallow (EI-AGH) and my father and I would fly there in the similar aircraft (EI-AGA) in which my father shared ownership. I took my usual place in the front cockpit and off we went in formation with George. Flying in the Swallow was something I always looked forward to. A graceful pre-war design that was built using several

My father, David 'Dave' Montgomery and his good friend, George Donohoe.

different engine combinations, it bore many similarities to a powered glider with its relatively high aspect ratio wings and graceful flight. Manufactured under licence from the German Klemm company, 'AFN' and 'AGA' were powered by the Cirrus Minor in-line engine rather than the Pobjoy engine that had powered the original design, and had a top speed of 90 mph and a landing speed of just 30 mph.

The day was perfect with very good visibility and in a short time we arrived at our destination and circled the prospective airfield before landing. I've never managed to discover where we had flown that morning but soon after we landed a member of a religious order, based adjacent to the field, came out to us and invited us to come in for a cup of tea. This we all duly did and strange as it may seem, although I cannot remember many other details of the building, I can still conjour up its smell, unique to premises that have been used for religious purposes for a long time. Tea and biscuits over, we were guided back to the aircraft through the walled garden of the establishment. My father commented on the flowers there and how much my mother, a keen gardener, would have liked to see them. Whereupon, our guide, a kindly priest, insisted that we bring some back to her. So it was that I took my usual place in the front cockpit of the Swallow that was now jam-packed with flowers. A short flight later, we were back at Weston and the flowers had been presented to my delighted mother. My father sent me to get the cushions I needed so that we could go up next in his Tiger Moth. I needed these because the cockpit of the Tiger Moth was deeper that that of the Swallow. Having collected the cushions, I ran eagerly back to my father, anxious to take the air in EI-AHJ, the Tiger Moth that he had bought the previous year.

Imagine then, my disappointment when he told me that he had been approached by one of his pupils and would take him for a short lesson before going for the flight with me. My father, who had qualified as a Flying Instructor in November 1955, took off in Tiger Moth EI-AGS, a machine that belonged to the Aero Club of Ireland, rather than his own aircraft, as the income for the lesson would go to the Club. His pupil was a young man called William Kenny, who was an advanced pupil. He had been a keen aeromodeller and like my father, was in love with flight and flying.

This was the last time I saw or talked to my father.

• • •

Even our dog was named after an aeroplane - this is 'Spitfire' -our beloved Wire-haired Terrier. And she was a Spitfire!

My father grew up in the Ireland of the 1930s. Ireland was a very different place then, impoverised by the War of Independence and the Civil War that followed and severely affected by the world trade recession and economic war with Britain.

David's father, George, my grandfather, had been a member of the Dublin Metropolitan Police and then a Harbour Policeman in Dublin until his untimley death from a heart attack in 1935. Undoubtedly, the times were hard for my father and his siblings growing up and perhaps it was no surprise that he found diversion from everyday life in aviation. My father kept numerous aviation scrapbooks and from these it's clear that flying and everything associated with it, occupied a very large part of his waking hours.

My father's collection of solid scale model aircraft, built without kits or in most cases, plans, using photographs in contemporary flying magazines. This war-time display was mounted to raise funds for the local Boy's Brigade in North Strand in which my father was a member.

My father also developed great skill as a modeller, building from scratch many solid scale models of the aircraft of the day. These were rarely built from plans and never from 'kits', being fashioned from side views and photographs in the aviation magazines he devoured. He was also talented as an artist and was able to paint on the 'markings' on his model aircraft rather than using transfers. (I have many of his drawings – almost invaribly aviation subjects with a small number of drawings of horses, in which he developed an interest in the period before he learned to fly). I'm also fortunate to have a photograph of his models set out on the living room table for an exhibition given to raise funds for the North Strand Boy's Brigade in which he was a sergeant. Its particulary fortunate that this photograph exists as the models shown were destroyed in a disastrous house fire in 1947, just before I was born.

My father had his first flight, aged sixteen, and taken in a DH 83 Fox Moth (EI-AAP) operated by Everson Flying Services, on Tuesday 3rd July 1934. He took off from Kildonan Aerodrome in Finglas on a short pleasure flight over Dublin city. This was a transformative moment and set him on the road that would

Red-letter day as my father takes his first flight in DH Fox Moth EI-AAP at Kildonan, Finglas. The date was Tuesday 3rd July 1934 and the flight was over Dublin.

define his life, and to a lesser extent, mine, even though I was still many years in the future. I have no doubt that from the moment of his first flight onwards, my father's burning ambition was to fly.

But first he had to find the means to allow him to do so – no easy task in the Ireland of the time where private aviation was the preserve of the very well-to-do. After several false starts he managed to establish a hardware and glass business in Dublin's Parnell Street, that was to thrive in the years that followed. My father had married my mother, Lily Magee, in the dark days of 1940 and I have no doubt that her support was an essential ingredient in my father's business success. Theirs was a marvellous loving relationship and created a happy environment into which my younger sister, Ruth, and I were born.

• • •

The afternoon wore on. There was plenty going on to keep me occupied as Weston was busier than usual owing to the 'At Home' event. Something that was popular on days like this were 'joy-rides' over the surrounding area and today Capt. Darby Kennedy was busy taking paying passengers up in the DH Dragon Rapide that carried eight passengers at a time. The first indication that something untoward had happened was when Darby Kennedy returned from one of these flights and as the passengers disembarked several of them were obviously distraught and one young woman was hysterical. It was then that we noticed for the first time a pall of black smoke rising into the air from the general direction of Lucan. Darby quickly took off again in his green-cowled Tiger Moth EI-AFJ. He had seen the burning wreckage of an aircraft during the pleasure flight and had diverted over it but was unable to recognise whose aircraft it was, so fiercly was it burning He now landed beside it but the wreckage had blazed so fiercely that nothing was recognisable. Ironically, the blazing aircraft had fallen onto a football pitch where a unit of the Dublin Fire Brigade were playing a football match.

Back at Weston a chill feeling spread through those present. I was to experience that feeling and the ominous silence that goes with it later in my life while at a motor racing event where there had been a fatal accident. But who had been involved? Most of the aircraft were now absent from Weston taking part in the cross-country competition that was part of the 'At Home' event. At that time very few small private aircraft in Ireland were fitted with radio comunications so there was no alternative for all the anxious friends and relatives but to wait as the aircraft made their way back one by one, oblivious to the tragedy that had unfolded. My mother, of course was amongst them.

She also had my sister to look after as well as me, and I was old enough to have some understanding of what had happened. During the hours that followed while we waited to learn to whom tragedy had befallen, my mother displayed the courage that she was called upon to display so many times in a difficult life. Several hours passed and the aircraft returned one by one. By late in the evening there were just two aircraft that had not returned. One belonged to Bob Magill and the other to my father.

My mother was very calm during this period of waiting. She comforted Bob Magill's girlfirend who had become very upset. Finally, after long hours of waiting, a Gipsy Major engine could be heard drawing closer. It was a Tiger Moth, but which one? Finally, it landed but even before then we knew it was my father who had been lost. I don't remember very much of what followed after the return of Bob Magill. I know my mother remained calm and concerned to shield my sister and I as best she could. Eventually, word came that the two bodies had been taken to Dr. Steevens' Hospital beside Heuston Railway Station (formally Kingsbridge). My memory of the journey is vivid, driven in my father's car by one of the Club members who stopped to buy cigarettes along the way. When we arrived at the hospital I was left to look after my sister outside the morgue, while my mother went inside. After what seemed an eternity, she returned, visibly shaken. Because my father was so badly burned, my mother was not allowed to see his body, and he was identified by the rings he had worn.

Some time later, we arrived home to our house in Baldoyle. My mother took charge of everything and when the visitors who had arrived with good intentions to offer their condolences had departed, we were finally left alone. My mother took me into her bed that night and asked me to put my arm around her waist. Only then did she allow herself to quietly cry.

• • •

With the perspective of the years that have passed, I can only marvel at the courage that my mother showed on this and other occasions in her life. She was just 34 years of age when my father died. She was left with two small children – one little more than a baby

My mother entered enthusiastically into her role as Patron of the Irish Parachute Club, of which my father had been a founder just two weeks before his tragic death. She is here delivering a short speech under the watchful eye of Freddie Bond in the clubs training facility at Weston aerodrome.

– yet she took over the running of my father's business and disposed of the nine DH Chipmunks my father had recently imported into Ireland. One might suppose that she might never have wanted to go near Weston again, yet knowing how much flying had meant to me, within a month or two we spent the occasional day there, where various club members, in particular, George Donohoe and Bob Magill, were kind enough to take me flying, Without doubt, what she was trying to do was to continue what had been our normal activity. Shortly afterwards, Freddie Bond of the Irish Parachute Club, invited her to become the clubs' patron. She did this with enthusiasm, knowing my father would have wanted her to accept the honour. It even led to her making a speech at an Irish parachute Club function, something that I know terrified this brave lady more than anything else.

In the years that followed I must have broken her heart, carrying my obsession with aviation through first aeromodelling and then powered flight lessons. When I began to be deeply immersed in competing in motorsport, I suspect she breathed a quiet sigh of relief, believing I had chosen a less dangerous activity. Little did she know!

• • •

The mishap that occurred when my father was taking a flight test in BA Swallow EI-AFN. Because of a communications problem with the aircraft, a situation arose where neither my father or the examining pilot were actually flying the aircraft, which flew gently (luckily) into a field in Mulhuddard, County Dublin.

My father had his first flying lesson on February 5th 1951, taking to the air in a BA Swallow (EI-AFN) with 'Darby' Kennedy at the controls. It was a twenty minute local flight and thereafter he logged at least one training flight each week. After a few weeks, tuition switched to a DH Tiger Moth (EI-AFJ), still under the instruction of Darby Kennedy. On January 20th 1952, with a grand total of 20 hours 40 minutes tuition he soloed in the Tiger Moth. Thereafter, progress was quck and he was certified competent to carry out cross-country flights on 29th June 1952. By now, it's noticable from my father's log book that he was flying several times a week. On 12th January 1953 he took off for a flight test from Collinstown with Captain Gordon Wade. There had been some doubt as to whether the flight test would go ahead as there was a problem with communication between the front and rear cockpit of the BA Swallow owing to an issue with the Gosport Tube. In the event, the decision was taken to proceed on the basis that Captain Wade would demonstrate the manouver he wished my father to carry out, and then my father would repeat it. Things proceeded without difficulty until they came to the procedure for emergency landings. Normally, this would involve trottleing back the engine without warning and then finding a suitable field for an emergency landing. Usually, the procedure was to 'open' up the throttle again just before landing and to climb away.

However, on this occasion, things became a little mixed-up, and it turned out that neither Captain Wade or my father were flying the Swallow. The result was that instead of the engine being used to abort the landing, the aeroplane flew gently into the ground, wipeing off its undercarriage and breaking the propellor. I imagine there were also some blushes from the two occupants...
The flight test was successfully repeated on 9th April in Swallow EI-AGA, once more with Captain Wade and on this occasion there were no unintentional heavy landings.

The author's first flight was taken in an Aer Lingus DC-3 over the City of Dublin on St. Patrick's Day 1949.

By now my father had accumulated 89 hours flight time and had flown several different aircraft apart from the Swallow and Tiger Moth, including Avro Cadet (G-ADIE), Piper Cub (EI-AFE), DH Dragon (EI-AFK) and Miles Messenger (G-AGOY). It's noticable from his log book that he was enjoying aerobatics and practiced them regularly. Also, by now I was regularly flying with my father, having made my own first flight on St.Patrick's Day 1949 at the tender age of two years and five months. The flight was a special flight over the St. Patrick's Day parade in Dublin city operated by Aer Lingus in a DC3 Dakota (EI-ACF). My father kept a Pilot's Log Book for me of all of my flights and in it he has recorded, *"Conditions bad – gusty – bumps: Passengers not allowed to undo safety straps during flight: Most passengers airsick."* Between then and April 1952 I had several flights in the DH Dragon (EI-AFK) piloted by Darby Kennedy and accompanied on several occasions by my mother as well as my father. July 15th was a memorable day as I made my first flight in a BA Swallow flown by my father. I was a few months shy of five and sat on my mother's knees in the front cockpit.

From then until his death in September 1956, my father wrote-up - first in a modified 'Parcel Book', and then in a official Weston Log Book – a record of my flying along with his own every week. Cross-country flights, navigation and the lessons he gave me are all recorded with his comments. Not surprisingly, these Log Books are today amongst my most treasured possessions.

Early days when I flew sitting on my mother's knees in the front cockpit of the Swallow EI-AGA, in which my father shared ownership as part of a syndicate.

While my father took every opportunity to encourage my interest in flying, both his and my Log Book include numerous references to cousins and school friends of mine that he treated to what was usually their first flight. Indeed, at one time he learned of the establishment of an Air Scout troop and made arrangements to take each of the boys up individually for a first flight. Perhaps the best example of his desire to inspire a love of flying was the story of Michael O'Brien, told elsewhere in this book. Suffice to say, either in taking people up for a first flight or through the weekly column he wrote in the *Evening Mail*, he never ceased trying to spread the infectious enthusiasm he felt for all things to do with aviation.

Sometime in 1954, my father, who was also the Honorary Secretary of the Aero Club of Ireland based at Weston, and others had the idea of staging an Air Display at Weston during 1955. The first Air Display in Ireland had been held as early as August 1910 when the members of the Irish Aero Club held an Aviation Meeting at Leopardstown race course, just eight months after Harry Ferguson had become the first to fly in Ireland. During the 1930s Ireland had been visited by the travelling Flying Circus of both Sir Alan Cobham and its successor, the CWA Scott Flying Display. Undoubtedly, the members of the Aero Club of Ireland felt that an Air Display at Weston after a gap of some twenty years would greatly increase the public's awareness and interest in private aviation in Ireland and plans proceeded over the winter of 1954/55.

The 1955 Air Display was held over the Whitsun holiday weekend and was an outstanding success attracting an audience estimated by the *Irish Times* to be in excess of 50,000, and was repeated again on 20th and 21st May 1956 to similar success. As Honorary Secretary of the Club, my father was deeply involved in the planning and organisation of these events and I even had a small role in the 1956 display. On that occasion – in an attempt to show that 'anyone' could learn to fly – I made several low level passes in the Swallow while my father held his arms outstretched from the rear cockpit to demonstrate that I

The Weston Air Displays captured the imagination of the Irish public - and the commercial world! This was Lemon's sweets press advertisement.

was in control.

Mention has already been made of the weekly 'Aero Club of Ireland' notes that my father wrote and that appeared in the *Evening Mail* newspaper. In an unattributed article about the history of the Leinster Aero Club (the successor of the Aero Club of Ireland) in the *Irish Air Letter,* the author wrote:

> *"To write a worthwhile article on any historic topic, good sources of information are essential, and here we are very fortunate. Starting in November 1954, a weekly column appeared in the Dublin* Evening Mail *newspaper, written by the Club Secretary, David Montgomery, under the pen name 'Icarus'. It appeared each Friday. These columns provide a fascinating history of Weston in the mid-fifties and well capture the atmosphere of the place and the following article is based on them".*

In our house, Wednesday night was when my father would sit down after his dinner at his writing desk to write the weekly 'notes' for the *Evening Mail,* always signed off as 'Icarus', and often with the salutation 'Happy Landings'. Like the author of the article in the *Irish Air Letter,* I have found the notes to have been an invaluable source of information in preparing this book. More than that, however, they have provided a reminder, if one were needed, of my father's infectious enthusism for flying and all things to do with aviation, and his desire to share that enthusiasm.

Little can he have imagined that sixty-two years after he first penned them, his notes would still be quoted.

• • •

After my Father's untimely death, Ernie Verso, the Treasurer of the by now re-named Leinster Aero Club took over as Honorary Secretary and continued to write the weekly notes under the ironic pen-name of Daedaleus, and also succeeded my father as the key organiser of the Weston Air Displays that continued in 1957 and 1958. My mother was invited by Freddie Bond to become the Patron of the Irish Parachute Club, which he, together with my father and George Donohoe, had established just two weeks before my father's death. My mother entered enthusiastically into the role which she continued to fulfill for several years. We also returned to Weston regularly for some time before other interests demanded our time and our visits became less frequent. Later, when I could afford it, I took flying lessons with Darby Kennedy at Weston. After one lesson in very turbulent conditions, I was surprised when Darby asked if I had my Student Pilot's licence as he considered I was ready to go solo. I had just four and a quarter hours tuition with Darby. So, all that time flying with my father more than a decade before must have had some effect. But at that point my hopes were dashed as having worn glasses for short-sightedness since I was fourteen, I failed the Student Pilot Medical as I did not meet the minimum standard of sight without glasses. Disappointed, I became involved in motorsport and in particular, circuit racing, where I went on to become an Irish national champion and to race successfully in Europe on an International licence. Not bad for someone who failed his Student Pilot Medical!

Smiling faces at the inaugural meeting of the Irish Parachute Club. From left: Founder members David Montgomery, George Donohoe and Freddie Bond. The Club was formed just two weeks before my father's untimely death.

Over the years, aviation has not been forgotten, and I've enjoyed gliding at Lasham in England and in the Austrian Alps. My memories of those days at Weston are very precious and whenever I fly, be it a commercial flight or in a glider or light aircraft, I always have an overwhelming sense of having come home again, when we climb through the clouds, something for which I will always be thankful for to my father and to Weston.

WESTON AERODROME

Weston aerodrome photographed around 1955. Darby Kennedy is over-flying in his green-cowled DH Tiger Moth EI-AFJ, while on the ground are (from left) a Pobjoy-engined Swallow, DH Rapide, Miles Gemini, Avro Cadet and Miles Messenger. The two open fronted hangers can be seen clearly while the building on the extreme right is the Aero Club of Ireland's club-house. To the left partially hidden by trees is Darby Kennedy's house. In the background is the 'lake', actually a broadening of the River Liffey that served as a useful landmark for pilots returning to Weston.

Darby Kennedy's Tiger Moth takes to the sky. An ex-RAF Tiger Moth, AFJ was registered in March 1950 and was in use almost daily until March 1966 when the registration was withdrawn and it is believed she was scrapped. Familiar to every visitor to Weston, Darby Kennedy's aerobatic displays in her were legendary.

A DH-89A Rapide EI-ADP, this aeroplane provided a first flight by means of a local 'joy-ride' for many, many members of the public at Weston and at various locations around Ireland. She was sold to the UK in April 1955 and subsequently was re-registered in France.

EI-AFJ

A fine photograph of Darby Kennedy with his Tiger Moth, EI-AFJ. This was the machine in which my father, following instruction from Darby, made his first solo flight on 27th January 1952.

Around the time that my father first started to regularly visit Weston aerodrome, this Percival Proctor EI-ACX, was one of the stalwarts of Darby Kennedy's fleet. First registered on 18th January 1947, it was eventually scrapped at Weston in July 1960.

Another view of Percival Proctor EI-ACX, but this time showing, in the background, the yard at Weston. To the left is Darby Kennedy's house while beyond it the large structure partially hidden is the main hanger. To the left of the main hangar was a shed that housed a Link trainer. To the right of it is a second smaller hanger while on the extreme right is the building that became the clubhouse of the Aero Club of Ireland after its formation in 1953.

Another view of Percival Proctor EI-ACX, probably taken around 1950.

This Pobjoy-powered British Klemm BK1 Swallow was one of several Swallows – both Klemm and BA versions - that operated from Weston. A classic pre-war design it was originally registered as G-ACMK, and it was first registered to Weston Limited on 25th March 1948, changing hands in 1955 before being owned by Vincent O'Rourke in January 1959. Its registration was cancelled in June 1960.

A very familiar sight at Weston during the time of the Aero Club of Ireland, this BA Swallow 2 was originally registered as G-AFGV before being registered in Ireland to Frank Murray in August 1960. After several changes of owner-ship it was withdrawn from use in May 1967, after which parts from it were used in the restoration of another Swallow EI-AFF.

An aeroplane that holds a very special place in my memories of Weston. It was first registered in Ireland as EI-AGA (previously G-AFIH) in June 1952 when my father was one of a syndicate of fliers who operated this aircraft. I first flew in this aircraft sitting on my mother's knees and afterwards did my initial tuition in her.

A lovely photograph of one of the BA Swallows overflying two Tiger Moths, the nearest of which unusually for an Irish example of the type has a fully-painted fuselage.

A fine air-to-air photograph of BA Swallow 2 EI-AGH taken by my father. This Swallow is being flown by George Donohoe who accompanied my father on many formation flights cross-country to locations throughout Ireland.

A second aerial photograph of EI-AGH. Originally registered as G-AFHH, this Swallow was re-registered in Ireland as EI-AGH in December 1953 to George Donoghue who sold her on in January 1957. Sadly, she crashed at Abbeyshrule in April 1959 and her registration was cancelled in February 1960.

In May 1955 a number of DH Tiger Moths were purchased from the Royal Air Force for use by the Aero Club of Ireland. This photograph was taken following their successful ferry flight from RAF Cosford via RAF Valley, on arrival at Weston. All suitably attired for the Irish Sea crossing with 'Mae Wests' they are from left: Vincent O'Rourke, John Kerwin, David Montgomery and George Donohoe.

WESTON PERSONALITIES

Percy William Kennedy, known to all as 'Darby', was Ireland's best-known aviator. After a career in Imperial Airways flying the HP42 biplane airliner and also the 'C' class flying boats on the routes to India, he returned to Ireland and established Weston aerodrome and Weston Limited in 1938. At Weston he combined four large fields to form the aerodrome and established a flying school using BA Swallow 2 EI-ABX, which had previously been registered to him in England as G-AFES. When private flying was suspended in May 1940 he became a pilot for Aer Lingus, becoming its Chief Pilot in 1945. In 1947, he resigned from Aer Lingus and decided to concentrate on developing Weston aerodrome and building up his flying school and charter business. In subsequent years, two DH89A Rapides were acquired, as well as two more Swallows and a Percival Proctor, but any attempts to establish an airline in opposition to Aer Lingus were swiftly halted by Government.

With the formation of the Aero Club of Ireland in 1953, Weston became established as the most important centre of private flying in Ireland, a status it continues to enjoy today. Hugely significant in the history of aviation in Ireland, Darby Kennedy imparted the gift of flight to thousands of airmen before his death at age 102 in May 2016.

George Donohoe was one of the founder members of the Aero Club of Ireland, He first flew in 1951 and made his first solo after just ten hours instruction. An electrical contractor, "in his low-wing Swallow monoplane, he flies to most parts of Ireland, and business acquaintances and friends never know quite when he will 'drop in'." *Navan born, married with a grown family, George was one of the most popular members of the club, in which he was also an instructor.*

Barry Eagan was the popular Chairman of the Aero Club of Ireland and was a member of a well-known firm of Dublin wine merchants based in St. Stephen's Green. He had first flown with Dublin Air Ferries in the days of Lady Heath at Kildonan aerodrome at Finglas.

Stephen Donohoe, brother of George, was another popular figure at Weston. He accompanied George on many of his cross-country flights throughout Ireland.

Their hobby is flying

Flying is the hobby of this mother and daughter, Mrs. Louise Lyons and Dublin Hospital nurse Judy Lyons. In their spare time they take a Tiger Moth up at Weston, Co. Dublin, H.Q. of the Aero Club of Ireland. They became members of the Club last year, and qualified to fly solo in the same week. Judy has 13 flying hours to her credit and her mother 30.

There were several women fliers at Weston, the best known of whom was Rosemary Kennedy, the eldest daughter of Darby and Joan Kennedy. Also particularly noteworthy were mother and daughter, Mrs. Louise and Judy Lyons. Judy was a nurse at the Adelaide Hospital in Dublin and both joined the Aero Club of Ireland at the same time, subsequently going solo on the same day.

'Nat' Preston, a farmer based at Kilmessan, Co. Meath, combined his interest in flying with competing in motor racing. He was a familiar competitor at the race tracks at Wicklow, at the annual Phoenix Park motor races and at Hillclimb events throughout the country, driving an MG. The inset photograph shows him at speed on the Phoenix Park circuit.

Ken Brown was Assistant Chief Flying Instructor with more than 2,300 hours of flying logged on nearly a score of different aircraft types. Ken served in RAF Bomber, Transport and Training Commands, in Europe, the Far East, Canada and the USA, flying single, twin and multi-engined aircraft, before returning to instructing on his first love – Tiger Moths. A Sales Manager with Rowntrees, he was greatly missed when he left Ireland to take up a post in South Africa.

Jack McLoughlin was a non-flying member of the Aero Club of Ireland and was one of the essential 'back-room' members essential to the success of any club such as this. A member of the Club committee, he was particularly involved in the series of Air Displays held at Weston.

Bob Magill was one of the most active of Aero Club of Ireland members, qualifying as an instructor, being an accomplished aerobatic pilot and also acting as the pilot for many parachutists at Weston. His Tiger Moth EI-AGT with red-painted fuselage was one of the most distinctive on the Irish register and this was eventually replaced by a DH Chipmunk T10s (EI-AJD) originally registered to Pearse Cahill of Iona Airways.

Father Augustus Ryan, a pupil of my fathers and one of several priests flying regularly at Weston. The most prominent of this group was Father Vincent O'Rourke, who was an experienced pilot and took part in the ferry flight of the Club Tiger Moths from RAF Cosford.

A very 'posed' photograph of Aero Club of Ireland members relaxing in the Weston Clubhouse. They include: David Montgomery, Steven Donohoe, George Donohoe, Kevin Murray and Ken Brown.

This British registered Avro Cadet Mk II was based at Weston for several years and distinguished by its all-black fuselage and silver wings and tailplane colour scheme. I recall flying in this aircraft several times with my father and my memory is of an aircraft that seemed very powerful compared to the Tiger Moth I was more used to. G-ADIE was built in 1935 and powered by an Armstrong Siddeley Genet Major 1 engine. It was registered to Republic Air Charters as EI-ALP in September 1960, T Cunnliffe in April 1961 and to John O'Loughlin in April 1964 when it was based in Castletown, Wexford, for many years.

A second photograph of the Avro Cadet, this time an air-to-air showing off its attractive silver and black colour scheme.

Freddie Bond, who together with my father and George Donohoe, would found the Irish Parachute Club based at Weston in September 1956, makes a parachute jump from the Tiger Moth EI-AHJ of Darby Kennedy. It was Freddy Bond's love of parachuting that saw the Irish Parachuting Club being formed and going from success to success.

When Freddie Bond, along with George Donohoe and David Montgomery, formed the Irish parachute Club in September 1956, no one had made a parachute jump here in over 20 years. Freddie Bond had become interested in parachuting in 1935, when as a boy of 12, he witnessed a descent by a member of Scott's aerial circus at the old racecourse outside Longford town. He joined the army in 1939 and was one of the first instructors posted to the new L.D.F.. Dismayed by the lack of opportunity to parachute, in 1943 he secured his release and joined the Parachute Regiment in England, volunteering for special service. In 1944 he was dropped into occupied France, operating there for several weeks as part of Special Operations Europe. He made 118 descents in battledress and ended the war as an instructor in the Parachute Regiment.

Following a lengthy illness, he returned to Ireland and with the formation of the Aero Club of Ireland saw the opportunity to establish sports parachuting in this country.

During the Summer of 1955 The Sunday Press *and* Daily Sketch *newspapers picked up a story from* Aersceala *- the Aer Lingus staff magazine - about a young boy whom staff members had noticed at the airport on numerous occasions. My father made contact with the boy through the* Sunday Press *and offered to take him for a flight at Weston. Michael O'Brien - the young boy in question - takes up the story:* " On arrival at Weston I remember meeting with a photographer from the *Sunday Press* who took pictures of us in the aircraft.
I also recall meeting with 'Monkey' Morgan who was sitting on a butter box reading a newspaper and he would later get airborne in his Auster EI-AGJ and fly with us where additional photographs were taken. We took off on the north-easterly grass strip and that wonderful experience is still clear in my memory to this day... My interest in aeroplanes had been there for some time prior to meeting Dave, however my first flight consolidated my interest and for which I will be forever grateful to Dave - and *The Sunday Press* for introducing us."

Michael went on to have a long and distinguished aviation career and today is still involved as Ryanair Board Director of Safety.

EI-AGA

Spectacular photograph of Michael's first flight over Maynooth. This photographs was taken by 'Monkey' Morgan from his Auster flying in formation with my father's BA Swallow.

VISIT OF THE USS SAIPAN TO DUBLIN

In July 1952 there was an unprecedented event in Dublin when the USS aircraft carrier, the Saipan*, visited the port. The* Saipan *berthed at Ocean Pier in the Alexander Basin. Eighteen aircraft were on-board when the carrier visited Dublin, although she had the capacity for fifty. For the visit, all of them were clustered at the stern with wings folded. The majority were Grumman Avengers and Hellcats and in addition there was a most interesting Piasecki HRP-2 Retriever helicopter. All of these aircraft were painted in a dark blue colour scheme apart from a single all-yellow SNJ Texan.*

My father flew over the carrier while it was entering Dublin port and afterwards visited it when the accompanying photographs were taken.

Some of the Grumman Avengers with wings folded on board USS Saipan.

The USS Saipan *in Alexander Basin. The carrier had a single straight flight-deck, this type just beginning to be replaced by an angled flight-deck at that time. In this photograph the full compliment of aircraft grouped together at the stern of the ship can clearly be seen.*

The twin-rotor Piasecki HRP-2 Retriever helicopter was unusual for the time. Note the folded rotor blades.

1

2

3

4

1. *Some of the Grumman Hellcats on board the* USS Saipan.
2 & 3. *Stern views of the* USS Saipan, *showing its complement of aircraft parked at the rear of the flight-deck.*
4. *Front view of the Piasecki HRP-2 Retriever helicopter.*

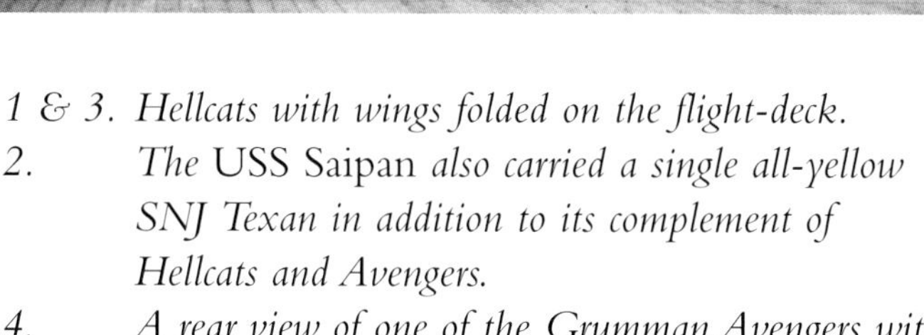

1 & 3. Hellcats with wings folded on the flight-deck.
2. *The* USS Saipan *also carried a single all-yellow SNJ Texan in addition to its complement of Hellcats and Avengers.*
4. *A rear view of one of the Grumman Avengers with the carriers superstructure in the background.*

ON THE BEACHES

During the Summer of 1954, my mother underwent a long spell in hospital, and during this time I stayed with family friends in Crossmolina, County Mayo. My father flew up in EI-AGA to visit me, accompanied by George Donohoe in EI-AGH. The two BA Swallows flew from Weston to Clifden via Galway and the Ox Mountains before making a shorter hop of 40 minutes from Clifden to Enniscrone where they alighted on the beach.

Their arrival generated considerable local interest and many locals visited the beach to view the two aircraft.

The two aircraft were left overnight on the beach. Many years later, when I was in my first employment, a colleague mentioned he was from Enniscrone, and I told him about my father's visit. The effect this had on him was totally unexpected as he told me how as schoolchildren they had been given the day off school to see the aeroplanes and how the event had begun a life-long interest in aviation for him.

In the late 1940s and early 1950s the Dragon and Rapides of Weston Limited were familiar sights on several of the beaches of Ireland where they would land to offer joy-rides. In this photograph, taken on Bettystown beach, EI-ADP is apparently about to take off, watched by a curious crowd of onlookers. I can also recall landing on Dollymount Strand with my father and George Donohoe in BA Swallows.

THE WESTON AIR DISPLAYS

Official programmes for the 1955, 1956 and 1958 Weston Air Displays.

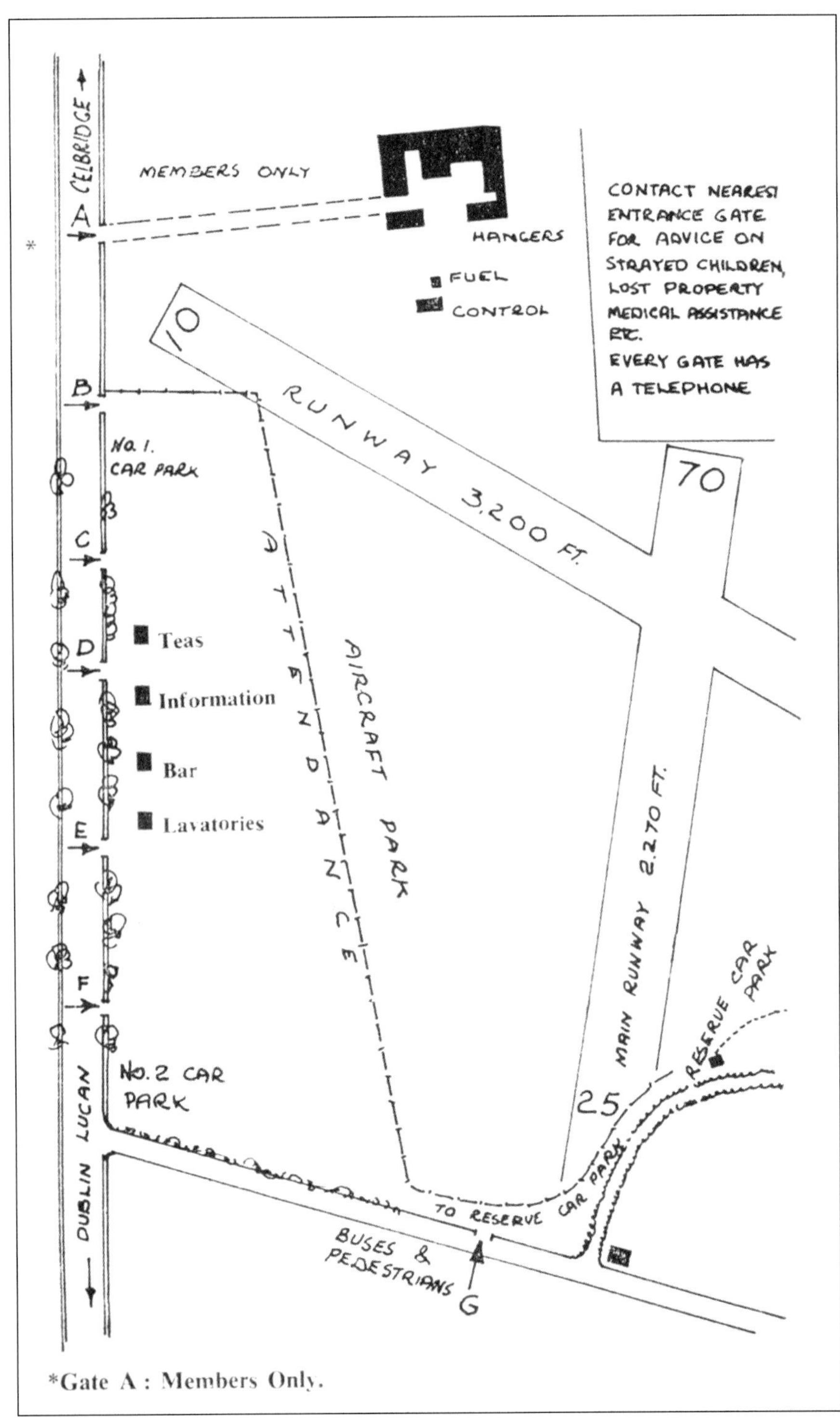

The layout of Weston aerodrome showing arrangements made for the Air Displays of 1955 and 1956.

An Tanaiste, Mr. William Norton TD, who officially opened the 1955 Air Display is shown the aerodrome plan for the event, by from left: Barry Egan, David Montgomery, 'Monkey' Morgan and Darby Kennedy.

One of several photographs used for publicity purposes prior to the first Weston Air Display in 1955, showing, planning the event, from left: Barry Egan, Darby Kennedy, George Donohoe and Rosemary Kennedy, daughter of Darby.

A photograph that was very widely used in the pre-event publicity for the 1955 Weston Air Display, showing my father adjusting the flying helmet of Rosemary Kennedy, Darby's eldest daughter. Rosemary, at 17, was already an accomplished pilot and gave a well-remembered display of spinning at the 1955 Air Display.

A familiar sight around Weston in the lead-up to the Air Displays were the formations of Tiger Moths and Swallows practicing formation flying in preparation for the event. In this photograph Tiger Moths EI-AGR and EI-AGS fly in close formation.

An unusual photograph of five of the Club Tiger Moths preparing for a massed take-off which they repeated in the 1955 Air Display to great effect.

Three Seafires of the Irish Air Corps led by Captain Tim Healy, gave a superb display of formation aerobatics, something that caused Spitfire ace Douglas Bader to comment, 'that it was the finest display of formation aerobatics I have ever witnessed.' *High praise indeed.*

The Irish Air Corps provided this static display Seafire at the 1955 Weston Air Display. It proved to be a major attraction not just for the public, but also for the Weston pilots. Here, George Donohoe and my father cast their eyes over the type which was then soon to be replaced by the DH Vampire in the front-line of Aer Corps aircraft.

Lieutenant Julian Bongeot, an instructor with the French Parachute Training School, about to take off with Darby Kennedy in the Avro Cadet during the 1955 Air Display at Weston. Lieutenant Bongeot made a delayed parachute jump from 12,000 feet that prompted Darby Kennedy to comment: ' He baled out at 12,000 feet and I thought from the look of things he was heading for Baldonnel. But, even though he had to go down through some cloud, he landed about 300 yards away from the point at which we hoped he would land - an astonishing performance.'

Swedish aircraft manufacturer, Saab, sent an example of their good-looking Safir 4-seater executive aircraft to the 1955 Air Display as a demonstrater. The Safir attracted a lot of attention and although one was ordered for an Irish owner, it was in fact cancelled before delivery.

One of the highlights of the 1955 Air Display was an appearance by one of the new Aer Lingus Viscount 707s that had been delivered to the airline the year before. Piloted by Captain RB Seigne, EI-AGI opened the display with a low-level pass before then demonstrating it's abilities with just two of its four engines operating. Aer Lingus was at the time celebrating its 19th year of operations and over two million passengers carried.

The 1955 Air Display opened in spectacular fashion with a low-level pass by one of the new Aer Lingus Viscount 707s. The BA Swallow in the foreground is George Donohoe's example.

In the second of these two photographs a portion of the vast crowd estimated by the Irish Times *at 50,000 can be glimpsed in the backgeound.*

All cleaned up for the show! The Irish Shell personnel who efficiently operated the refuelling at Weston were, from left to right: Des Ryan, Brendan Foster and John Lally.

Several demonstrations of formation flying were given by Aero Club of Ireland members in the Air Displays. This Tiger Moth formation is overflying one of the gliders that took part in the demonstration of gliding by the Dublin Gliding Club, who also used Weston as their base for operations at that time, operating from an enlosure at the far end of the airfield.

DOUGLAS BADER AT WESTON

Douglas Bader, the famous World War II Air Ace who lost both his legs in a pre-war flying accident, flew into the 1956 Weston Air Display in his Miles Gemini aircraft, accompanied by his wife, Thelma.

Douglas Bader was at the time Head of the Aviation Division of the Shell Company and was photographed at Weston with his wife Thelma, and (on left) JVB Tighe, Shell Dublin Branch Manager and J F Dixon, Assistant General Manager, Irish Shell Limited.

A smiling Douglas Bader signs autographs for young enthusiasts at the Air Display. Bader had a reputation as a forceful and difficult character but the author has memories of a kindly man, who encouraged his interest in their conversation about flying and aeroplanes and left a strong impression.

THE SHELL ROSE BOWL TROPHY

At the end of the 1955 Display, a presentation was made by William Norton TD., on behalf of the Irish Aero Club, of the Shell silver rose bowl trophy to David Montgomery in recognition of his work in promoting sport aviation in Ireland. Looking on is Capt. Kelly-Rogers, the famous Chief Pilot of Aer Lingus. Some fifty years later the author had the great pleasure of presenting the same trophy to that years winner in a ceremony at Weston.

DUTCH BALLOONISTS AT WESTON

Dr Jo and Nina Boesman, members of the Balloon Club of Holland brought one of their balloons, here seen in flight over Europe, to Weston for the 1956 Air Display. Sadly, what was expected to be one of the highlights of the Air Display, had to be cancelled due to strong winds on both days. Although the weather was very unsuitable the Dutch balloonists did their best not to disappoint the huge crowd and made a tethered ascent to 100 feet in the balloon PH-BL, which was claimed at the time to be the largest in the world.

Although the Dutch balloonists failed to fly un-tethered at the Weston Air Display, they presented my father with this hand-painted commemorative plate and jug depicting their balloon in flight over Dublin's Four Courts. Their tethered ascent was the first time a balloon had been flown in Ireland since JJ Dunville early in the twentieth century.

AIR DISPLAY PARACHUTISTS

Peter K Rayner, of the Irwin Parachute Company, who took part in the 1955 Air Display.

Lieutenant Julian Bongeot, an instructor with the French Parachute Training School, made a parachute descent at the 1956 Air Display, impressing Darby Kennedy with his accuracy.

Christian-Ladouet, who made a parachute descent at the 1956 Air Display.

In addition to these parachutists, Rene Vincent, a celebrated French parachutist, made a drop at the 1956 event, thrilling the crowd as he used three consecutive parachutes while dropping from 4,000 ft., a feat he repeated at the 1958 Display.

MARTIN-BAKER EJECTOR SEAT DEMONSTRATION

One of the highlights of the 1956 Weston Air Display was the appearance of a RAF Gloster Meteor Mk.7 that demonstrated the newly introduced Martin-Baker Ejector Seat by ejecting a dummy during a low-level pass at Weston. History had been made in this aircraft when on 3rd September 1955 Squadron Leader John Fifield had safely ejected at a speed of 120 mph from a height of fifty feet. His parachute deployed at thirty feet and he made a safe landing. The Meteor was flown at Weston by Captain JED Scorr, seen in this photograph on arrival at Collinstown. This was the first time a jet aircraft had appeared at an Irish Air Display.

DH CHIPMUNK TEST FLIGHTS AT RAF COSFORD

Early in 1956 my father negotiated the purchase of nine DH Chipmunk trainer aircraft from the Royal Air Force. His intention was to provide a modern fully-enclosed trainer for the members of the Aero Club of Ireland. On June 6th and 7th I was fortunate to accompany him and George Donohoe to RAF Cosford to conduct test flights of the chosen aircraft before arranging to ferry them back to Ireland. All of the Chipmunks were test-flown at RAF Cosford and I had the unforgettable opportunity of flying from an operational RAF base in company with North American F86 Sabre and DH Vampire aircraft. In this photograph George Donohoe is strapping me into the front cockpit before one of the test flights.

Two of the Chipmunks at RAF Cosford. Their Irish registration marks were crudely painted onto them at this stage in prepration for the ferry flight to Ireland. The Chipmunks involved were: EI-AHR, EI-AHP, EI-AHT, EI-AHW, EI-AHU, EI-AHV, EI-AHY, EI-AJB and EI-AJA.

Having test-flown the Chipmunks, George Donohoe and my father travelled to RAF Speke on June 18th in the Miles Gemini EI-AHN piloted by Lord Kildare, with the intention of ferrying the first two aircraft back to Ireland. Bad weather grounded them at Speke until 22nd June when the ferry flight was successfully accomplished. A further ferry flight was made on 27th June. Later the same day they returned to RAF Speke with several other club members in DH Dragon EI-AFK flown by Captain Kennedy to continue ferrying the remaining Chipmunks to Ireland. Three aircraft set out in formation from RAF Speke on the following day but bad weather over the Irish Sea caused them to lose sight of each other. There was some concern when they became overdue at Collinstown but all three landed safely with only George Donohoe reaching Dublin Airport as planned. My father landed in Ballygunner in Co. Waterford and the remaining aircraft in Carlow. The photograph shows EI-ALC at Collinstown, now with correctly painted registration marks.

At around the same time Pearse Cahill of Iona Airways also imported several ex-RAF Chipmunks. one of which was purchased by Bob Magill and registered as EI-AJD. This photograph shows Bob's Chipmunk in flight and looking very smart in her post-RAF colour scheme.

A famous passenger in EI-AJD. Mike Hawthorn, then the F1 World Drivers Champion, was treated to an aerobatics demonstration by Bob Magill in his Chipmunk. Sadly, having become the World F1 Champion while driving for Ferrari, and having announced his retirement from the sport, Mike Hawthorn was killed in a road accident shortly after his flight with Bob Magill.

VISITING COLLINSTOWN

Signpost to Everywhere! This sign stood outside the entrance to Collinstown. The iconic Desmond Fitzgerald designed terminal building with the original Control Tower on top is visible in the background.

A photograph of Collinstown taken in the early 1950s when the taxi-ways had just been added to the original paved runways. On several occasions I flew into Collinstown with my father and Darby Kennedy in Tiger Moths. Joining the circuit (the Tiger Moths had no radio fitted) we landed on the grass and taxied to park in front of the Control Tower. Cups of tea and biscuits in the Control Tower usually followed. Different times!

On Tuesday 25th May 1948, a Royal Air Force Gloster Meteor touched down at Collinstown. This aircraft, a Meteor F Mk.4 (RA444) was the first jet aircraft to visit the airport and was a demonstration by the British Government of the type to the Irish Air Corps. Interestingly, this was a regular RAF aircraft attached to 257 Squadron and piloted by Flight Lieutenant Scannel, and not a Gloster demonstrator. The demonstration on the following day was reported by the press: "The plane roared across the airfield at 600 mph with vapour trails flaming from the engines, it rolled in the sky and dived directly on the airfield from altitudes of up to 15,000 feet, with a final run over at full speed 30 feet above the ground". *Further demonstration flights were made at the Curragh and Gormanstown.*

1

2

3

4

1. *One of two B-50Ds of USAF Strategic Air Command that visited Dublin on Saturday 18th November 1950. Powered by four Pratt and Whitney R-4350 radial engines, they were the largest aircraft to have visited Collinstown up to that time.*
2. *Converted Handley Page Halifax bombers were regular visitors to Collinstown in the late 1940s and early 1950s. Their first visit was in August 1948 when an example of the type flew a cargo of plums from Paris to Dublin.*
3. *Aer Lingus acquired two Airspeed AS 65 Consuls in 1948 from Aer Rianta Teoranta that were used for crew training and charter work. EI-ADB was cancelled from the Irish register in June 1949 and later crashed at Leopoldville in the Belgian Congo, while EI-ADC was sold to the Karachi Aero Club in 1953.*
4. *C-47s, the military version of the Douglas DC-3 Dakota, were frequent visitors to Collinstown and nine ex-USAAF C-47s were purchased by Aer Lingus.*

1

2

3

4

1. *In March 1950, a TWA DC-4 named 'Gates of Suez' (N86571) landed at Collinstown having been diverted from Shannon while en route from Gander to Paris. After re-fueling it returned to Shannon which had re-opened by then.*
2. *One of three Savoia Marchetti SM.82s that arrived in Collinstown in August 1951, to transport pilgrims for the Dublin Diocesan pilgrimage to Lourdes. Although operated and owned by the Italian Air Force, the aircraft belonged to 36 Storfuo (Squadron) and were painted in the colours of the Order of St. John of God of Jerusalem.*
3. *An unidentified Aer Lingus DC-3 Dakota, showing the early almost all-metal finish carried by the airline.*
4. *A Convair 240 visited Collinstown in September 1954. Belonging to KLM it carried the President of the airline, General I Alier, who was on a tour of all KLM stations.*

1. *A Viking of Trans World Charter photographed in the early 1950s when the type was a frequent visitor to Collinstown.*
2. *A real puzzle! This radial engined DC-3 has a third engine installed in its nose. At a later date three engined turboprop conversions were made to the DC-3 but this predates them.*
3. *A rare visitor to Collinstown, a Boeing 377 Stratocruiser of BOAC.*
4. *One of five Bristol 170 Freighters operated by Aer Lingus between1952 and 1956. This example is EI-AFQ.*

1

2

3

4

1 & 2. Two photographs of a graceful Trans World Airlines Lockheed Constellation. TWA Constellations were infrequent visitors to Collinstown but Air France examples of the type were also regular visitors and of course, for a period, several were bought by Aerlinte for their proposed transatlantic route.

3 & 4. In July 1950, the band of the USAAF arrived in Collinstown as part of a European tour in four SAF Fairchild C-82 Packets operated by the 60th Troop Carrier Group based at Frankfurt's Rhein-Main air base.

The band and their equipment arrived from Bovington and after playing in Dublin's Theatre Royal flew out the next day to Frederickshaven for their next engagement.

In August 1952, Collinstown was visited by a USAF RF-80 Shooting Star jet fighter aircraft. My father and Darby Kennedy flew over to the airport, having been told of the arrival of this exotic visitor by friends in the control tower. The plane was based near Munich, and was the reconnaissance version of the fighter. It carried the serial 58466 on its tail and FT-466 on the nose. It seems Darby Kennedy couldn't resist a closer look at the workings of its jet engine!

The following year, in June 1953, a flight of four USAF F-84G Thunderjets on a navigation training flight flew into Collinstown. The jets, based in Chaumont in France, were from the 48th Fighter Bomber Wing. An Irish Press *report described their arrival:* 'With vapour trails streaming like banners behind them, a flight of faster-than-sound planes whistled over Dublin Airport at 11.30 am on Thursday morning, banked, circled the airfield three times and then dipped their wings and glided gracefully down. The F-84 Thunderjets had arrived from Chaumont, 250 miles south of Paris, having completed the 660 mile journey at a cruising speed of 560 mph in 90 minutes. Officials and airport technicians streamed out to the tarmac to watch the planes give the traditional salute as they came in. One by one they banked suddenly until they seemed to stand upright on their wing tips, then just as suddenly they had rolled away at right angles and were flying in line again.'

A TIGER'S TALE

The remarkable journey of DH Tiger Moth EI-AHJ

EI-AHJ is a De Havilland 82A Tiger Moth that was manufactured by the Morris Motor Company in 1943. It was given the Royal Air Force registration, NL984 and its construction number was 86414, Code Number RCU-W.

The newly built aeroplane was allocated to 20 MU Aston Down on 4th January 1944 and issued to Elementary Flight Training School Burnaston on 5th September 1944, and subsequently passed to 19 Flight Training School at Cranwell in 1945, 22 EFTS Cambridge on 10th April 1947 and 22FTS Cambridge on 26th June 1947.

She made a forced landing at Town Mead Field, Waltham Abbey on 21st September 1948, when her engine dropped a valve. A rocker bolt failure during climb out from a practice forced landing at Cambridge on 17th April 1949 resulted in a real forced landing two miles from the airfield. Subsequently, she was routed to 12 MU Kirkbride on 12th May 1950 and RAF Valley Station Flight on 31st August 1954. She was then transferred to non-effective stock on 13th April 1954 and ended her RAF career when she was sold to Weston Limited on 26th October 1955 and registered as EI-AHJ on 21st September 1955.

On 27th October 1955, EI-AHJ was sold to my father, J David Montgomery. The inset photograph shows my father, clearly delighted with his acquisition which still has its RAF marking and also its new Irish registration marks. My father, most often accompanied by the author, continued to fly EI-AHJ right up to his untimely death at the end of September 1956.

J Farrell

Following my father's death EI-AHJ was sold by my mother to T Kerr Jnr., on 6th November 1956. He continued to use the aircraft until 30th August 1958 when she was re-registered to J Farrell, based in County Roscommon. The registration was subsequently cancelled on 1st December 1969. During this period EI-AHJ fell into dis-repair and was damaged in a storm when the accompanying photographs were taken, in the second of which her wings had been removed.

Following the cancellation of her Irish registration, she was sold to B Sheridan and exported to the United States. He in turn sold her to Eugene L Stringer of Tucson, Arizona who registered her as N8722.

On 22nd June 1970 she was on the move again - this time to James E Ardy in Phoenix, Arizona. Several days later, on 30th June 1970, ownership was changed to Andy's Antique Aeroplane Rental Inc.. In 1971 the aircraft was re-built by 10.71 at Phoenix to qualify for an Experimental Category Certificate of Airworthiness, which was granted on 5th November 1971.

On 19th October 1972 she was sold to John B Croft of Roseville, California, who retained her until March of 1976.

Tom Sumner - in front cockpit - of Seattle, became the next owner of this already well-travelled Tiger Moth on 15th March 1976. Tom completely rebuilt the lower wings using stack sawn ply ribs - a technique applied to American DH 60 Moth production during the 1920s - at an estimated total weight penalty of 1lb per wing panel. This disadvantage was outweighed by an immense saving in repair time and effort. Subsequently, a Certificate of Airworthiness application was made on 17th January 1979.

Operating from a 1500 ft strip at Martha Lake on 25th August 1979, the engine lost power on take-off and poured out black smoke. N8722 pancaked into a clearing, breaking the new starboard wing and rotating the undercarriage into the starboard fuselage side. Repairs were undertaken in Seattle against an agreed payment of an MG TC sports car!

Tom Sumner, who had nick-named N8722 'Olivia', enjoyed her company for some forty-one years before finally deciding that the time had come to pass her to a new custodian at the end of 2017.

1. *Tom Sumner carried out a superb restoration and re-build of N8722, changing her colour scheme to the post-war over all yellow of a RAF trainer of the 1950s.*
2. *'Olivia' on take-off.*
3. *A fine photograph of 'Olivia' showing Tom's careful restoration to full effect.*
4. *N8722 was based near Seattle during Tom's ownership, where his Golden Era Motors restored classic motor cars such as this supercharged Napier-Railton.*

N8722 passed into the ownership of Don Drake in March 2018. Based near Buffalo in New York State, Don made the bold decision to fly his newly acquired Tiger Moth from Seattle to his home base at Akron Airport, a journey of 2,400 miles that would involve crossing the Rocky Mountains. This photograph was taken at Missoula, Montana, and shows (on left) Don Drake who was accompanied by Dennis Borkowski, just before setting out to fly through Rogers Pass to exit the Rocky Mountains.

Over the Rockies. The waviness in the photograph is due to the prop pressure pulse rocking the camera. The total lack of anywhere suitable for an emergency landing is apparent. Thankfully, N8722 never missed a beat in her 2,400 mile journey.

1. *The lush countryside of Western New York. By this stage of the flight, Don had learned to take the photographs without the distortion due to prop buffeting.*
2. *Home base at last! Akron Airport was a welcome sight at the end of this great adventure.*
3. *Trails, mountains and clouds. Don reported that the flight was 'tense but also beautiful'.*
4. *N8722, safely in her hanger at journeys end.*

EI-AHJ/N8722/'Olivia''s current owner, Don Drake, at the end of her epic journey from Seattle to Akron. During the journey she flew 2,400 miles at an average speed of 80 mph (lower that anticipated because of unexpected headwinds), flew 30 hours with 18 stops and consumed 30 quarts of oil. The journey took two weeks and a day to cross the continent.

THE WEEKLY AERO CLUB OF IRELAND NOTES IN THE *EVENING MAIL*

"On the Dublin to Celbridge road there is an ordinary farmhouse gate, which opens surprisingly on to an aerodrome. The path from the gate leads to a farmhouse, twists through a chicken run and comes suddenly upon the chickens and the aeroplanes. In this setting, open-fronted hangers, the Tiger Moths, Swallows and Rapides, the small club house and the angular petrol pumps are not out of place. They are out of another time, perhaps, reminiscent of the pioneering days when aviators flew for the pure love of flying and an aerodrome was any flat field from which an aeroplane might take off".

David Montgomery

THE AERO CLUB OF IRELAND NOTES

At Weston Aerodrome last week-end the icy winds failed to keep the "hardy annuals" grounded, and there was quite a lot of flying activity. At one period air traffic was so heavy in the circuit that yours truly had to orbit twice whilst awaiting a turn to land.

Dr. Paris Panayotou was there in his new all-metal Cessna 180 cabin monoplane in which he plans to fly over six thousand miles to South Africa later in the month. The coldness of the day did not worry Paris however, whose aircraft is fitted not only with a very efficient cabin heating system, but with half a dozen radio aids, about two dozen I-don't-know-whats, and I am sure had my examination been thorough enough I would have found at least one of the proverbial kitchen sinks.

The annual general meeting, held on Monday last at the Clubhouse, was well attended. Mr. Barry Egan presided. The following officers were elected—President, Captain P. W. Kennedy; Vice-President, Colonel P. Quinn; Hon. Sec., D. Montgomery; Hon. Treas., E. Verso.

Several amendments were made to the rules. We were honoured by the presence of Mr. Denis Greene, President of the Irish Aviation Club, and after an address it was agreed to seek affiliation to the Irish Aviation Club, nominating Mr. Ken Brown as our representative.

Subscriptions for 1955, due since Jan. 1, are already coming in.

Enquiries re membership to the Hon. Sec., David Montgomery, "Mornington Lodge", Baldoyle, Co. Dublin. — "**Icarius**"

Every Wednesday evening my father would sit down at his writing desk and compose his Aero Club of Ireland Notes for inclusion in Fridays edition of the Dublin newspaper, the *Evening Mail*.

His first notes appeared in November 1954 and the last Notes on Friday September 28th, just two days before his untimely death. To call these words written to record the activities of the Aero Club of Ireland 'Notes' is hardly to do them justice. As other commentators have written, they not only provide an unparalleled insight into private flying in Ireland at that time, but also they reflect the author's infectious enthusism for flying and his desire to share his experience as widely as possible.

Consulting my Father's Notes while writing this book has been for me a wonderful voyage of discovery. Cross-referenceing his Notes with his Log Book – and also with the Log Books he kept for me – has opened a window on my Father's aviation experience that I never expected to find. It has also become apparent to me how much we shared in my short time with him and his clear wish that I should share his love of the skies. In that he succeeded and I know that many others also were influenced to a career in aviation or just to take to the skies by the words he wrote each week.

So, what follows is a short selection of some of the most interesting of his writings. I hope you enjoy them as much as I have*. For the sake of clarity, I've re-typed the Notes here included.

* *It is hoped to publish the complaete 'Notes' at a future date.*

INAUGURAL NOTES - NOVEMBER 1954

Hello Folks, - In these, our first notes, I hope each week to bring you into the crew room and introduce you to some of the club's personalities and aircraft, give you a brief resume on the previous week's flying and the coming weeks programme, perhaps even let you in on our plans for 1955, some of which are really ambitious to say the least, for instance a two-day National Air Display and Pageant but more about that later.

For the record, I should tell you that the Aero Club of Ireland was founded in 1953 by a handful of flying enthusiasts. Its object "*the advancement of aviation in Ireland, with particular emphasis on private flying*". Membership is now over sixty, thirty of whom hold Student Pilots' Licenses, whilst a dozen hold Private Pilots' Licenses. The Private Pilots' License, as a matter of interest, entitles the holder to fly in more than twenty countries throughout the world. The standard of flying is kept high under the eagle eye of Captain 'Darby' Kennedy, who probably has more flying hours logged on light aircraft than any other pilot in these islands.

If you have never been to Weston Aerodrome (its out by Lucan, only eight miles from Nelson Pillar) you should come out some Saturday or Sunday and see the lads (and lassies) in action. You might even be tempted into taking a "joy ride" or even a trial lesson. All interested in joining the Aero Club, either as flying or non-flying members, can have full particulars by writing to - **The Honorary Secretary, Mr. David Montgomery, "Mornington Lodge," Baldoyle, Co. Dublin,** or look out (or should I say "up"?) for him when you visit Weston Aerodrome.

So, until next week, "*Happy Landings,*" - ***"ICARIUS"***

Club members at Weston.

• • •

UNUSUAL WEATHER – SHELL FILM SHOW – AIR DISPLAY PLANS - 'MONKEY' MORGAN

Unusual weather last week-end gave Weston Aerodrome smooth flying conditions. Whilst the country outside a three-mile radius was subject to thick smog, with cold high winds beyond the fog belt, at Weston the Club pilots operated from a snow-covered aerodrome, where little or no wind prevailed. There was much flying activity, and when dusk fell on Sunday afternoon all sojourned to the club-house, where most members had arranged to meet friends and visitors for the successful film show that followed. The film *"Fifty Years of Powered Flight"*, was particularly good, and the Shell people are to be congratulated on a fine production. By the way, look out for a good aviation film, *"The Bridges of Toko-Ri"* coming to a Dublin cinema this week.

A general meeting is scheduled to take place at the Clubhouse on Monday next at 8 o'c. Full attendance by all members is requested, and an open discussion on club affairs, the coming air pageant set for Whit weekend, and the Continental trip for later in the year is included in the agenda.

Major 'Monkey' Morgan.

Crew-room Personality this week is six feet three inches tall, 35-years old Major Alexander Campbell Morgan, D.F.C., R.A., popularly known to one and all as "Monkey." Joining the Royal Artillery shortly after the outbreak of the late war, Monkey did his initial training on Magisters. About this time the first Auster Aircraft was being developed for military work, and the then Lieutenant was assigned to carry out most of the development, this involved amongst many other things, flying 150 hours and making 500 landings during the first month. Most of his two thousand odd hours logged has been spent on Austers in many climates, the U.K., Germany, North Africa and Italy, where the R.A.F. thought enough of him to make an award of the Distinguished Flying Cross, an unusual honour for an Army pilot. His training as an Army Observation Post fitted him well for his present occupation of Aerial Photographer and Charter Pilot. As proprietor of Airviews Ltd., he flies all over Ireland, photographing farms, factories, houses, housing schemes, land reclamation schemes, air surveys, topical news, etc. He was responsible for many of the fine Press photos of the recent disastrous Dublin floods. As charter pilot, his three seater Auster cabin mono-plane is available for flights (almost at a moment's notice) to any part of these islands and the Continent. Holder of an Instructor's Rating, he is a keen club member, and serves on several committees. Last year he captained the Aero Club of Ireland team which flew to the Channel Islands to compete in the International Air Rally there, against more than sixty competitors from half-a-dozen countries. The team won third place. This was the first time that the Republic of Ireland was represented at an International air meeting and they acquitted themselves nobly. When the occasion permits, he is accompanied on flights by his charming wife and little girl, Jennifer, both keen air travellers. In spite of his size, Major Morgan is quiet and unassuming, but is one of those people who, immediately absent, is missed. Glad to have you with us, Monkey. Happy Landings.

Weston Aerodrome is 7½ miles from Nelson pillar, out by Lucan on the main Dublin – Celbridge Road. Inquiries re membership to the Hon. Sec. David Montgomery, Mornington Lodge, Baldoyle, Co. Dublin. – **"ICARIUS"**

• • •

3rd June 1955 – THE 1955 AIR DISPLAY – JULIAN BONGEOT – PETER RAYNER – CAPTAIN TIM HEALY – ROSEMARY KENNEDY – BACK-ROOM BOYS

At Weston Aerodrome last week-end I felt proud to be a member of the Aero club of Ireland. Proud to have as my friends such good types as Darby, George, Rosemary, Ken, Barry, the Toms, Bobs and Ernies and the many too numerous to mention who put so much work into what turned out to be the biggest and best air display ever to be seen in this country, the popularity of which was such that all the roads leading to Weston just could not cope with the traffic and thousands of prospective spectators were disappointed.

Lieutenant Julian Bongeot.

WAR VETERAN

About eighty thousand people saw the star of the show, the dashing Lieutenant Julian Bongeot of the French Air Force jump from 12,000 feet, delaying his chute release until less than 2,000 feet from the ground to capture the hearts and admiration of the vast crowd. I met the gallant officer and found it hard to realise that at 24 years, this unassuming young man is a veteran of the Indo-China and Tunisian campaigns and has more than 2,000 drops to his credit, some of which took place under the fire and stress of war.

Capt. Peter Rayner of the Irving Parachute Co., who did the precision (if somewhat less spectacular undelayed) drop from the Auster is another of that very fine band – the Parachute Soldier. He, too, knows what it is to drop into battle under enemy fire. To Aer Lingus Captain Singh's crews we are indebted for their very fine Viscount demonstration. The Air Corps Spitfire Flight led by Captain Tim Healy thrilled everyone with their high-speed formation and fighter tactics flying, whilst Captain Louis Tracey in the Chipmunk did not disappoint in the "request aerobatics" item. What a great pity we see so little of these very fine Army pilots of which we all felt so proud last Sunday and Monday.

AEROBATIC MANOEUVRE

The Saab Safir's fully aerobatic qualities were capably demonstrated by that firm's pilot with the unpronounceable name (his Christian name which sounded something like "Ceylon" is the only part I can remember). This chap aptly demonstrated every aerobatic manoeuvre in the book, and many not in the book, yet practically all his flying took place within the boundaries of the aerodrome.

Our friends in Dublin Gliding Club carried out their item in the smooth manner we expected from them and are to be congratulated. Our own pilots too acquitted themselves nobly, Rosemary Kennedy's spiral dive from 5,000 feet followed by a loop thrilled spectators, whilst the Skippers aerobatics in a Tiger were done as only he can do them. In the obstacle race 'the obstacles' presented none to the pilots whose enthusiasm and agility outweighed the ability of the Course Marshalls to keep track of what was happening or who won, but nobody seemed to care, a good time being had by all.

The marquee dance each night was successful to say the least and when the scene was surveyed by the Display Committee on Tuesday morning they just stood around shaking each other by the hand and talking about the bigger and better one we are going to have next year.

TRIBUTES TO HELPERS

I heard more than one pilot however pay tribute to those back-room boys who do so much work and get so little of the limelight, "Chiefey" Pat O'Hara and his ground crews. It's a lot to say that every engine started on schedule and that no aircraft was grounded for any reason whatsoever. Other backroom folk who must not be forgotten were the ladies of the Social Committee who under Mrs. Donohoe toiled so hard under very difficult conditions to help the club. To the stewards, marshals, firemen, ambulance service, Gardai, Knights of Malta, Irish Red Cross, S.J.A.B., Boy Scouts etc., and the very many willing voluntary workers who contributed so much to the success of the day, I can only humbly say, "Well done."

WEEK-END FLYING

The Air Display Committee will meet on Monday next at the Clubhouse at 8 p.m. Flying is back to normal next week-end. The many visitors who were unable to avail of the joy flights at the Display can do so at week-ends and the queue will be smaller. If you did not avail of the special facilities that were available at the Display for joining the Aero Club, you may do so now. Full particulars may be had from the Hon. Sec., David Montgomery, Mornington Lodge, Baldoyle, Co. Dublin. **"ICARIUS"**

4th November 1955 – FERRY FLIGHT OF EX-RAF TIGER MOTHS – RENOWN OF CAPT. KENNEDY – "ANGELS ONE FIVE" FILM SHOW

North American Sabre aircraft at Speke Airport.

As I start to write these notes I am standing in the Meteorological Office at Speke Airport, Liverpool, looking out on weather that spells OUT for our planned flight to Dublin. Standing beside me are the Skipper, Capt. Darby Kennedy, Alan Ross and Cyril Murray. Cyril, by the way, is cultivating a very distinguished looking beard and we have already renamed him 'Sailor' Murray. Yesterday afternoon we collected three Tiger Moth aircraft from R.A.F. Station Cosford and flew them in formation to Speke, where strong head-winds and approaching darkness compelled us to rest for the night.

INTERESTING VISIT

At Cosford where a lot of modification test flying is carried out, we spent an interesting time examining the various machines which included Spitfires, Wellingtons, Balliols, Provosts, Austers (both Lycoming and Gipsy engine versions), Chipmunks, several marks of Ansons and a Pembroke. On the flight from Cosford we flew the 'Sailor' Murray flew the lead machine with the Skipper in the other cockpit combining the duties of Flight Commander and Master Pathfinder. Yours truly flew No. 2, whilst Alan Ross flew No. 3. En-route several R.A.F. machines came close enough for us to see the grinning face of the pilot turned towards us.

WAR VETERAN

At Speke we were given a grand reception and the freedom of the airport, due more than anything else to the popularity of the Skipper and the high esteem with which he is held there. He flew Aer Lingus machines in and out of Speke during the War years and is known to one and all as 'Darby.' At Speke too, we had an opportunity of examining at close quarters some late marks of swept wing Sabre Jet Fighters, which had just flown in from the U.S. via Iceland, and were destined for service with the R.A.F. On Thursday morning we left Speke and flew in perfect conditions to Collinstown Airport, taking one hour and fifty-five minutes. This flight, incidentally was the first light aircraft sea crossing for Alan and Sailor, who must now "stand a round" in the Clubhouse.

FILM DRAM'

On Friday last the film 'Angels One Five' was very well received by an appreciative audience of Club members and friends. On Friday next, 11th November, another film of drama in the air will be shown at the Clubhouse, together with a supporting programme of aerial shorts. I have not as yet details of the feature film but I understand it will be up to the same standard as 'Angels One Five.'

On Sunday last poor visibility over most of Ireland restricted most of the flying to circuits and bumps, although George Donohoe and Prince Michael did fly down to Waterford in the Prince's Messenger, returning to Weston before dark.

Details of the P.P.L. examinations have just come to hand. Full information will be had from the notice in the Clubhouse. Applications must be completed by all intending students on or before next weekend. Will all interested please contact David Montgomery now. I repeat now.

WEEK-END PROGRAMME

Improving conditions promise plenty of flying over the week-end, but the days are getting shorter so get out early. If no car don't forget Bus No. 67 passes the gate. Visitors welcome – flying available to spontaneous fliers. – **"ICARIUS"**

• • •

December 16th 1955 – COLD SNAP – 'BATTLE ZONE' FILM SHOW - CHILDREN'S PARTY – THE SHELL TROPHY

Over last weekend the glass was falling steadily: bad sign for Aero Club pilots. On Saturday the cold snap had a feeling of dampness and impending rain, which manifested itself by Sunday morning, continued steadily throughout the day and well into the night closing Weston Aerodrome to all air traffic. No aircraft whatsoever got airborne on Sunday to the disappointment of the flying types who retired to the Clubhouse for some "hanger" flying, and to watch a special impromptu afternoon showing of the film scheduled for Sunday night. The feature film "Battle Zone" with a supporting programme was well received.

The film show, plus card games and rings recently supplied by the Social Committee were in use for the first time and helped pass what might have otherwise been a flat afternoon. The Social Committee can do much to hold the types together in dull weather but much more effort and co-operation (to say nothing of individual keenness to work and help others) is needed from all concerned. However, the Committees only new, and probably, as it were having teething troubles.

Very few realise the importance of a good strong (and well supported) Social Committee, not only in Aero Clubs, but in any type of organisation where voluntary workers are required. Still fewer realise the amount of effort put into organising even such a small item as a Film Show, to say nothing of such events as the Christmas Social, with special guest artists, etc., arranged for Monday next, 19th instant (8 to 1) at the Clubhouse. Admission 5/-, members may introduce as many friends as they wish.

CHILDREN'S PARTY

To-morrow (Saturday) at 2.30 in the afternoon the Children's Christmas Party at the Clubhouse. Santa will arrive by air some time later to greet the kiddies, shake hands, have a sing-song and if we're lucky distribute presents.

The Aero Club's representatives Capt. Kennedy and David Montgomery attended the meeting on Thursday last week of the Powered Flying Committee (Chairman George Donohoe of the Private Owner's Section) where many items of momentous importance were discussed including the drawing up of rules for the Shell Trophy. A handsome

Waiting for Santa in the Weston Clubhouse.

Silver Rose Bowl is at present held by David Montgomery. It was decided that the Trophy should be awarded annually to the best all-round amateur pilot in Ireland. Commercial pilots and Flying Instructors not being eligible to compete. Only qualification necessary to enter the competition (there is no entry fee) is production of a valid Student or Private Pilot's Licence, and paid-up current membership of any Irish Light Aeroplane Club (i.e. Aero Club of Ireland, Shannon Aero Club, Newtownards Aero Club etc.). Marks will be awarded for un-hangering and starting up procedure, detecting and remedying snags, spot landings, cross-country flying, map-reading, navigation, and general good airmanship.

FINALS

The finals will be run, or should I say, flown off, probably in September next, which will give the pilots plenty of time to concentrate on the competition after the Air Display in May. Tomorrow and Sunday at Weston Aerodrome, Club Pilots will again be in the air flying to their hearts content, whilst various types of flying, aerobatic and cross-country, trial, instructional flights etc., will be available to members of the general public from 10/- a flight. The aerodrome is 7½ miles from Nelson Pillar, out by Lucan, on the main Dublin-Celbridge Road. Bus No. 67 from outside McBirneys stops at the gate. – **"ICARIUS"**

• • •

April 27th 1956 – THE FIRST SUCCESSFUL GROUND LEVEL EJECTION – THE 1956 AIR DISPLAY ON WHIT WEEKEND – FORT DONOHOE – AIR CORPS VAMPIRES

One of the 'Attack on Fort Donohoe' props.

On a lonely English aerodrome, one cold day last September, Squadron Leader JS Fifield, D.F.C, A.F.C., made history when he demonstrated for the first time a successful "live" ejection at ground level from a high-speed jet aircraft. Seated in the rear cockpit of a twin jet Gloster Meteor the gallant Squadron Leader as the "guinea pig" simulating an injured pilot flying at ground level started the release mechanism of the latest Martin-Baker fully automatic Ejection Seat, which shot him up into the air, clear of the machine, there the mechanism automatically parted him from the seat, and opening his parachute brought him safely to the ground.

Squadron Leader Fifield has been ejected at all levels up to 40,000 feet, but the one we are particularly interested in is the ground level ejection, for on Whit Sunday and Monday next (three weeks from now) at Weston Aerodrome the Martin-Baker people will demonstrate for the first time in Ireland an ejection at ground level from a modern high-speed jet aircraft.

JETS FOR AIR CORPS

The Martin-Baker seat ejection demonstration is particularly interesting in view of the fact that the Jet Vampires with which the Irish Air Corps are about to be equipped will be fitted with this latest safety apparatus. Potential Air Corps "Jet Jockeys" should be more than a little interested in the demonstration.

One of the seventeen items on the Flying Programme is down as a demonstration flight by the French S.I.P.A.

"Fort Donohoe" has apparently grown in strategic importance since last Whit weekend, for at this year's show the outpost will be defended by sterner stuff. Fighters will support the ack ack defences, and the wounded will be evacuated by air. I hope the bomber pilots know where to put the bombs.

Another "first" this year will be an Air Race, full details of which have to be worked out.
The bright evenings and smooth flying conditions are helping pilots to work into teams for Club items. All pilots hoping to participate must give names now to the Chief Flying Instructor, and pass efficiency test before being allowed to fly in the Display.

Members who complained of the high cost of last years' Air Display have an opportunity of helping to keep down expenses. The ways they can help will be outlined by Capt. Kennedy. All interested in joining the Aero Club should write to the Hon. Sec., David Montgomery, Mornington Lodge, Baldoyle, or look him up when next you visit Weston. **"ICARIUS"**

• • •

IDEAL FLYING WEATHER – RANALD PORTEOUS – THE AUSTER AIGLET – CREWROOM PERSONALITY BILL KENNY*

A steady 5-10 knot wind, coupled with good visibility gave flying conditions at Weston Aerodrome last Sunday, that can be described only as ideal by all privileged to get aloft. After Saturday's complete clamp down with rain (precipitation the Met boys called it) Sunday's glorious sunshine brought members to Weston from places as far away as Sligo, Kilkenny, Mullingar and Dundalk, and kept the Dublin Hills reverberating to the sound of Gipsy and Cirrus engines, sweet music to the ears of a pilot. Many visitors sampled "Trial" lessons from 20/- each, and from reports to hand I understand that more than one has been bitten by the "bug" (urge to fly). Many others, including several children had pleasure flights over Dublin and the surrounding countryside.

BA Swallow EI-AFN being readied for take-off.

From the Auster Aircraft Co. of England, whose Chief Test Pilot, Ranald Porteous, will demonstrate the fully aerobatic Aiglet at the coming Whit Air Display, I have just had news of their new model "J/1N" which they are constructing specially for Private Owners and Flying Clubs. Basically, the same as the Autocrat, it will have the more powerful 130 h.p. Gipsy Major engine, giving it a maximum speed of 126 m.p.h. indicated Air Speed, and a cruising speed of 105 m.p.h. I.A.S. consuming 6 ½ gallons of fuel per hour. The take-off run with a 5 m.p.h. wind is 135 yards, landing ditto, 125 yards. With an initial rate of climb of 710 ft. per minute, she takes 8 ½ mins. to reach 5,000 ft. With accommodation for a pilot and two/three passengers, this dual control high wing monoplane is just what the doctor ordered, or should order if he is a pilot. Delivery at present is 10-12 weeks. Priced at £2,000, a special discount of £100 will be allowed to Aero Club members.

* *Sadly, Bill Kenny was to die along with my father when Tiger Moth EI-AGS broke up in mid-air over Esker, Lucan, in September 1956.*

KEEN STUDENT

Crew-room Personality this week is Dublin-born Bill Kenny, who on Wednesday last at Weston Aerodrome made his first solo flight. Aged 23, Bill, who helps in the family Grocery Stores in Crumlin, had never taken flying instruction until he joined the Aero Club last summer. An apt pupil, Bill would have soloed months earlier but had to discontinue training owing to illness.

Always a keen student of aviation, he has been making model aircraft as long as he can remember and has won several aeromodelling contests. His second love is motor-cycling. Bill Kenny is at present doing the course in the "Tech" for the Private Pilots' Licence examination and hopes to qualify this year. Glad to have you with us, Bill. Happy Landings.

Flying helmets, Gosport tubes and goggles are again available from the Hon. Sec., who informs me that as many of these items are in short supply, and likely to remain so, all interested in doing so should equip themselves without delay.

On Monday next the Flying Committee will meet again at 8.00 in the clubhouse. Next week-end as usual flying available to all and sundry, but, get out early and help to keep 'em flying. – **"ICARIUS"**

• • •

"DAEDALUS" – RAF COSFORD – CHIPMUNK T10 TRAINERS – BOB MAGILL AND NAT PRESTON – LADY PILOTS – EASTER LANE - JUDY LYONS

While the worthy "Daedalus" was busy deputising for me writing last week's "Notes" yours truly was up in the bright blue yonder over R.A.F. Station Cosford test flying Chipmunk T10 Trainers destined for Weston Aerodrome. Delivery to Weston will probably take place next week.

Vampires at RAF Cosford.

In company with fellow Pilot-Instructor George Donohoe who did a considerable amount of the test flying, Engineer Pat O'Hara who examined and certified the machines for flight, and Bobbie Montgomery as "erk" we spent a most interesting few days at Cosford, not only flying these beautiful low-wing, fully aerobatic, all metal, air conditioned dual controlled, two mile a minute trainers, but watching the comings and goings at this vast maintenance depot, which is now closing down as such and is being turned into a Mechanised Transport Unit, maintaining only one type of aircraft. What type? Chipmunks, of course!

VARIED TYPES

Apart from Chipmunks we saw many marks of Spitfires, Vampires, Meteors, Balliols, Prentices, Oxfords, Ansons, Bristol Freighters, Dakotas and others including a Sycamore helicopter. We met the Station Commander, our old friend Squadron Leader Boardman, and the new C.O.S./L Matthews who put us at ease on any pros and cons. A former C.O. from Cosford S/L Gill is now Station

Commander at Aldergrove.

Back at Weston for the long week-end Bob Magill's chest looked swollen wearing his newly earned gold Private Pilot's Wings. Congratulations Bob, also to Nat Preston who recently obtained his P.P.L. and is now entitled to wear the pilots brevet. Ken Smith and Cyril now only need to complete their cross-country logs to qualify for their wings, whilst the popular lady pilot Easter Lane has the distinction of being the first girl in Ireland to pass the technical examination for the P.P.L. since the new I.C.A.O. international standards were set up. Hurry up Easter, you can become the first lady private pilot to qualify in Ireland.

LADY PILOTS

Amongst the lady pilots Rosemary Kennedy is doing most of the flying but I look forward to seeing more of Judy Lyon, Rosanne Anderson and Kathleen Ball-Dodd now that the hospitals examinations are over. We have missed Judy at Weston these past few months but she has not been wasting her time. Last week at the Adelaide Hospital where she is a nurse she won a gold medal for being the best nurse in the hospital, in addition to getting first place in medicine and in surgery. Judy made history last year when she flew her first solo on the same day as her mother. Congratulations ladies, happy landings.

This weekend at Weston Aerodrome, out by Lucan, on the main Dublin – Celbridge Road, flying instruction, trial flying lessons, and pleasure flights available to all and sundry. The Tiger Moth costs 20/- while pleasure flights in the 8-seater Dragon are from 7/6. Try one and see what you think. All interested in joining the Aero Club should write to the Hon. Sec. David Montgomery, Mornington Lodge, Baldoyle. – **"ICARIUS"**

• • •

PLEASURE FLIGHTS OVER DUBLIN – TRIAL LESSONS – ABBEYSHRULE AIR RALLY – GREEK MYTHOLOGY

An almost continuous downpour with high winds over last weekend reduced flying to a minimum at Weston Aerodrome, grounding Club Pilots for all but a few short bright intervals. Since Monday, however, a weak ridge of high pressure has improved the situation to such an extent that flying now ends only with darkness. Speaking of darkness Notam No. 35 01 1956 just to hand gives notice that on and from 22nd instant Dublin Airport will be open 24 hours daily.

The DH Dragon, joy riding mainstay of Weston activities.

With the 8-seater Dragon again available for joy riding the public are flocking to Weston at week-ends and in the evenings for short hops and pleasure flights over Dublin. These trips over Dublin, lasting fifteen to twenty minutes are marvellous value at 10/- a seat, and the shorter flights over Lucan at 5/- a seat, are instrumental in introducing hundreds of people to air travel, putting flying within the reach of everyone at a rate even less than it was pre-war.

TRIAL LESSONS

At Weston, too, all day during day-light hours flying instruction and trial lessons by qualified instructors takes place in 2-seater Tiger Moth aircraft. It is not necessary to be a Club member to have a trial lesson and it is an excellent way of finding out how one feels in the air. Re Abbeyshrule Air Rally scheduled for Sunday next, there is now some doubt about the suitability of the field for use as an aerodrome, and all Club pilots are urged to contact their instructor before proceeding to the Rally.

I have been taken to task by a scholar of ancient Greek mythology, Mr. Grogan of Dublin, over my spelling, or should I say mis-spelling of my pen name? The situation, it appears was worsened by my satellite "Daedalus" who writes this column when yours truly is missing from the fold. "Daedalus", it appears, spelled "Icarus" correctly, but then proceeded to spell his own name wrongly. Our thanks and apologies, Mr. Grogan, to me Greek has always been double-Dutch. Happy Landings. – **"ICARUS"**

• • •

September 14th 1956 – FARNBOROUGH TALES – NO. 54 SQUADRON RAF HUNTER AEROBATICS - AN IRISH AIR CORPS AEROBATIC TEAM?

The boys are back from Farnborough with tales of their adventures equal to any of the pioneers. The most epic flight was made by Pilot Tom O'Rourke, who with Noel Boylan as navigator made the eight hundred and odd miles flight there and back in George Donohoe's open two seater B.A. Swallow monoplane. Flying expenses for the flight came to less than £15, including carnet (aircraft triptych) and landing fees. Who said flying was a rich man's hobby?

BA Swallow EI-AGA in which my father and I spent many happy hours.

AT FARNBOROUGH

Their vivid description of events at Farnborough fill all with envy. "Sonic Bangs" were completely absent at this years' show although most of the Jet military aircraft demonstrated were capable of supersonic speeds. Of the brilliant acts, Neville Duke's faultless demonstration of the Hawker Hunter; Jan Zurakowski's "zurabatics" in the CF1-100; Ron Beaumont's display in the Camberra; "Cats-eyes" Cunningham's flying of the beautiful Comet 3; Roland Falk's slow rolls in the mighty delta winged Vulcan Bomber; Peter Twiss's demonstration of the needle-nosed Fairy Delta 2, which will probably be the first British aircraft to fly at speeds in excess of 1,000 m.p.h.

There was also Ronald Porteous precision aerobatics in the Aiglet; Ted Tennant's tiny green-painted "Gnat" capable of diving through the sound barrier, and the able demonstrations of nearly sixty others of the finest Test Pilots in the world, faded into insignificance, and were soon forgotten when, with an ear-splitting scream four Hawker Hunters in box formation from the crack No. 54 Squadron of the Royal Air Force, came on to put on a show of formation aerobatics that brought the crowd to its toes with loops, turns and rolls that showed teamwork second to none.

R.A.F. PILOTS

This was not the first time that this team from No. 54 Squadron had demonstrated its prowess. These four pilots (four ordinary types, just like you or me) have flown at air displays all over Britain and the Continent and have competed against crack teams from the U.S.A.F. and the world's air forces. There is no finer advertisement for the R.A.F. than these four young men who are doing the thing we all love so much – flying.

Having met these men and having heard so much about them got me thinking – why could not our Irish Air Corps develop a team such as 54 Squadron? In the Air Corps we have some of the finest pilots (fear their comrades might think I was "shooting a line" prevents me from mentioning names) whose individual flying records leave nothing to be desired, and who, I am sure would be proud to show the flag on Air Corps machines in any corner of the world.

INTERNATIONAL ARENA

It would not be necessary to fly in supersonic jets to enter the international arena. The French Air Force had a team of biplanes performing at international air shows up to the end of last year. Piston engine "Spitfires" which are the current Fighter equipment of the Air Corps are considered by many of today's jet pilots to be the finest fighters ever built. The extra speed of the jet fighter in many ways defeats its own purpose by using up and requiring too much sky for aerobatics.

We have an Army Jumping Team which holds its own amongst the world's horsemen. We have the pilots too. Why not an Air Corps crack aerobatic team? Then we could say we fly the flag. Only once in the past twenty years, at our air display last Whit Weekend did the public get an opportunity of seeing Air Corps pilots in action. This is not enough. If these chaps were good enough to be the "first line of defence" in the Emergency, surely they are entitled to some limelight now.

FLYING INSTRUCTION

Will Student Pilots undergoing flying instruction, please note that the course in ground school for the Private Pilot's' Licence starts in about one week. Application for inclusion should be made immediately to the Hon. Sec., David Montgomery, as additional names will not be added once the class commences.

All interested in joining the Aero Club should drop out to Weston Aerodrome sometime during daylight hours and have a chat with Capt. Kennedy, David Montgomery or any of the boys (or girls). They will be only too happy to let you have the full "gen." Flying instruction, trial flights, aerobatic flights and pleasure flights available at all times. If no car, bus No. 67A from outside McBirney's stops at the gate. – **"ICARUS"**

• • •

September 21st 1956 – 'AT HOME' EVENT – SPOT LANDING EVENT – FARNBOROUGH – KEVIN STREET PPL COURSE – INAUGURAL MEETING OF THE IRISH PARACHUTE CLUB

The unusually large crowd at Weston on Sunday saw Club pilots practicing aerobatics and spot landings for the "At Home" set for 30th inst. The Aero Club's representatives, Capt. Kennedy, D. Montgomery and G. Donohoe, on the Irish Aviation Club's Flying Committee will meet to-night in an endeavour to include the "Shell" Trophy for competition on same date.

A happy group with the Pobjoy-engined Swallow in the background.

I understand that about a dozen entries have been received for the Spot Landing event, but the Aerobatics competition is not getting the support it deserves from such a large Club. How about it chaps? We won't be looking for world championship standards, and the entrance fee is only half a dollar,

Congratulations to Ken Smith and Cyril Murray, who last week made the trip to Farmborough sharing the duties of Pilot/Navigator in Cyril's Tiger Moth EI-AHK. The thrill of seeing the world's greatest Air Display was only one of the events in an interesting trip, the details of which I have to learn. The two airmen visited half a dozen aerodromes in the U.K. including Fair Oaks where they renewed acquaintance with J.P. O'Hara, former chief engineer at Weston.

PILOTS COURSE

There are some vacancies for the Private Pilots Licence Winter Course starting shortly in Kevin St. Technical Schools. The fee for the complete course is £5. It is the best value ever offered to any potential or practical pilot, and should be sent to the Hon. Sec., Aero Club, with details of hours logged as soon as possible.

A more enthusiastic group of young men and women it would have been hard to find than the 65 clerks, soldiers, students, tradesmen, professionals, shop assistants, civil servants, ex-Paratroopers, nurses etc., who turned up on Monday at Aer Lingus Clubrooms for the inaugural meeting of the Irish Parachute Club.

It was addressed by the two founders of the Aero Club. The Hon. Sec. and Flying Instructor, David Montgomery, and Aero Club Parachutist Freddie Bond, outlined the objects of the Club. On the platform was Aero Club founder member and Flying Instructor, George Donohoe.

WINTER TRAINING

Having the benefit of Instructors, Pilots and parachutes, a group of prospective committee members are endeavouring to secure suitable premises for indoor training during the winter months. Venue and time of next meeting will appear in next "Aero Club Notes." Anyone anxious to serve on a committee is asked to attend a meeting on Wednesday next, 26th inst., at 8 p.m. at Aer Lingus Clubrooms, Beresford Place.

This week-end at Weston Aerodrome, I urge all interted in flying to get out as early as possible. Flying time is shortening and it is now dark to fly at 8 p.m. All interested in joining the Aero Club should write to the Hon. Sec. David Montgomery, Mornington Lodge, Baldoyle, Co. Dublin. For appointment to fly phone Lucan 435. – **"ICARUS"**

ACKNOWLEDGEMENTS

There are many people I'd like to thank for their help in putting this book together and whom I talked to about this project down the years: Michael O'Brien, Michael Traynor, Tom McCormack, Jane Magill, Barry Eastwick, Pat Gibbons, Tom Sumner, Don Drake, Catherine Greene, John and Steven Donohoe, Lisa Kelly and, of course, Alan Pepper.

Photographic Credits: David Montgomery Archive: Pages 2, 3, 11, 12, 13, 15, 16, 17, 18, 20, 23, 25, 26, 27,28, 29, 30, 31, 33, 34, 36, 37, 38, 39, 40, 42, 45, 54, 55, 56, 57, 58, 59, 60, 61, 63, 70, 71, 73, 77, 79, 84, 85, 86, 93, 94, 95, 96,n87, 88, 89, 90, 93, 94, 95, 96, 97, 98, 99, 100, 101, 102, 103, 195, 116, 121, 123, 124, 126, 128. **John Horgan:** 21, 22, 32, 46, 47, 48, 67, 68, 74, 115. **Irish Press:** 35, 65, 66, 69, 72, 83. **Jane Magill:** 44, 91, 92. **Barry Eastwick:** 41. **Major Morgan:** 49. **Irish Times:** 50, 119. **Sunday Press:** 51, 52. **John C Cooney Collection:** 62. **Irish Shell:** 78, 80, 81, 82. **Ken Tilley Collection:** 104. **Alan Pepper:** 120. **Pat Gibbons:** 106. **Tom Sumner:** 107, 108. **Don Drake:** 109, 110, 111, 112.

Published by Dreoilín Specialist Publications Limited,
Glenstal Mews, Westminster Road, Foxrock, Dublin D18XW81, Ireland..
Telephone +353 87 418 4360 e-Mail: dreoilin95@icloud.com

Distribution by Gill. Telephone: +353 1 500 9500
Trade enquiries (Ireland) to Butler Sims Limited. Telephone: +353 1 406 3639
Trade enquiries (UK and Overseas) to Star Book Sales. Telephone: +44 1235 465521

First Published in September 2018

ISBN: 978-1-902773-32-2
A CIP record for this title is available from the British Library

Design Alan Pepper Design, set in Bembo and printed in Ireland by GPS.

See us on Facebook 

Happy Landings!